Coconut's

TOP-SECRET

Code Book

Tricky, fun codes for you
and your friends

★ American Girl™

Published by Pleasant Company Publications
Copyright © 2005 by American Girl, LLC

Questions or comments? Call 1-800-845-0005,
visit our Web site at **americangirl.com**, or write to
Customer Service, American Girl,
8400 Fairway Place, Middleton, WI 53562-0497.

Printed in China
07 08 09 10 11 LEO 10 9 8 7 6 5 4

American Girl™ and its associated logos, Coconut™, Licorice®,
and the Coconut and Licorice designs and logos are trademarks
of American Girl, LLC.

Editorial Development: Therese Maring, Trula Magruder

Art Direction and Design: Camela Decaire, Chris Lorette David

Production: Kendra Schluter, Mindy Rappe, Jeannette Bailey, Judith Lary

Illustrations: Casey Lukatz

Pssssst!

Coconut has a secret she wants to share.
Actually, she has lots of secrets—secret codes!
With Coconut's **Top-Secret Code Book**, you
can learn **14 codes** and practice decoding
Coconut's special sayings. You'll find Decoder
Cards you can share with friends so that they
can understand your messages, too. You even
get **Secret Strips** to tear out and use for sending
super-tiny messages.

Have fun cracking the codes!

Your friends at American Girl

Doodle Decoder

Each doodle in this code begins with the letter of the alphabet it stands for. Try these doodles, or draw your own.

A:
B:
C:
D:
E:
F:
G:
H:
I:
J:

K:
L:
M:
N:
O:
P:
Q:
R:
S:
T:

U:
V:
W:
X:
Y:
Z:

4

Decode this Coconut message:

START

EVERY DAY

WAGGING

YOUR TAIL.

Share this version of the Doodle Decoder with up to four friends! Use the Decoder Cards from the back of this book.

5

Coco Latin

You may have heard of pig Latin, but this version of the coded language has a Coconut twist!

Here's how it works: If the first letter of a word is a consonant, move it to the end of the word, and add the letters **oco**. If the consonant sound is made of two or more letters, like *sh* or *ph*, move all of them.

> **girl = irl + g + oco = irlgoco**
> **shine = ine + sh + oco = ineshoco**

If a word begins with a vowel, just add *oco* to the end.

> **octopus = octopus + oco = octopusoco**
> **egg = egg + oco = eggoco**

Coco Latin works best when it's said out loud. Practice with your friends. It gets funnier the faster you can speak it!

6

Say this message aloud! Then translate it from Coco Latin to English.

practicin

Racticingpoco
ithwoco aoco riendfoco
akesmoco anythingoco
oremoco unfoco!

Silly Spaces

For this written code, put a space after each vowel rather than after each word. For example:

A na pple a da y ke e psthe do cto ra wa y

means

An apple a day keeps the doctor away.

Decode this Coco joke:

What animal makes the best decoder?

A du ckbe ca u
se i tca nqu a
ckthe co de s!

Secret Signs

Don't want to send a written message in code, but need to keep something secret? Try this tip!

Whether your friend's across a room, in the library (*shh!*), or standing in line, you can still communicate with signals.

Blinking your eyes three times could mean "Call me!" You could also tug an ear, grab your elbow, or hold up a pinkie finger.

Common messages you might
want to have signals for:

Meet me after class.
Where are you going?
We need to talk soon.
I'll call you later.
Hang in there!
You're the best.

By the Numbers

Write out the alphabet. Underneath, put the numbers 1 through 26, starting where only you and your pal will know. We started at "H." When you write your message, use the numbers instead of the letters.

A	B	C	D	E	F	G
20	21	22	23	24	25	26

H	I	J	K	L	M	N
1	2	3	4	5	6	7

O	P	Q	R	S	T	U
8	9	10	11	12	13	14

V	W	X	Y	Z
15	16	17	18	19

Decode this Coconut message:

A̲   t̲ r̲ u̲ e̲
20   **13-11-14-24**

f̲ _ _ _ _ _
25-11-2-24-7-23

_ _ _ _ _ _
12-13-2-22-4-12

_ _   _ _ _ _
21-18   **18-8-14-11**

_ _ _ _
12-2-23-24.

 Share this version of By the Numbers with up to four friends!
Use the Decoder Cards from the back of this book.

"i" Spy

When writing secret messages, slip an "i" after each vowel to disguise your words.

Seiei? Iit's eiaisyi!

Decode this Coconut message:

Friieinds airei
eiveiryiwheirei—
yoiui juist haivei
toi loioik.

Wheel of Secrets

Use the decoder wheel to reveal one of Coconut's golden rules.

Decode this Coconut message:

$$\overline{10}\ \overline{18}\ \overline{19}\ \overline{10}\ \overline{15}\ \overline{22}$$

$$\overline{18}\ \overline{9}\ \overline{6}\ \overline{20}$$

$$\overline{10}\quad \overline{8}\ \overline{9}\ \overline{18}\ \overline{28}\ \overline{25}\ \overline{6}\ \overline{21}$$

$$\overline{28}\ \overline{10}\ \overline{19}.$$

Share the Wheel of Secrets with up to four friends! Use the Decoder Cards from the back of this book.

Puzzling Pattern

This code uses a tic-tac-toe pattern and X shape to hold the letters of the alphabet. To encode a message, draw the lines and dots that appear around each letter, and leave the letter out.

A	B	C
D	E	F
G	H	I

J
K X L
M

N	O	P
Q	R	S
T	U	V

W
X · · Y
Z

Decode this Coconut message:

⊏⊡⌐⊏⊡⌐⌐⊐⊏⊓⌐⌐

⋀⌐⊐⊃⊡⌐　⟨⌐⊏⊡

⌐⊐⋁⊡−⌐⌐⌐⌐⊡⟨⟨

⊓⊡⊡⌐⊐⌐ !

 Share the Puzzling Pattern with up to four friends! Use the Decoder Cards from the back of this book.

Book It!

For this code, you and a friend each need a copy of the same book—one you are reading for class would work. Open the book and look on any page for the words you want to use in your message. Now you just have to tell your friend where to find each word! Here's what to do:

First give the number of the page where the word is found, using three digits:

341 means the word is on **page 341.**
012 means the word is on **page 12.**

Next give the number of the line where the word is found, using two digits:

03 means the word is on the **third line.**
29 means the word is on the **twenty-ninth line.**

Finally, give the number for the place of the word in that line, using two digits:

02 means it's the **second word** in the line.
16 means it's the **sixteenth word** in the line.

So if the word **"call"** is on page **341** on the **third line,** and it's the **second word,** the code for it would be **3410302.**

Decode the message below by looking up the numbers in the **Top-Secret Code Book!** The headline on each page—like "Book It!" on page 20—counts as line 1.

0061404   0110402   0160301

21

Dots & Dashes

Morse code was used to send messages by telegraph. Put a slash / after each letter, and place each word on a new line.

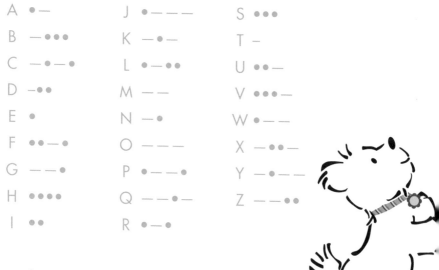

A •—

B —•••

C —•—•

D —••

E •

F ••—•

G ——•

H ••••

I ••

J •———

K —•—

L •—••

M ——

N —•

O ———

P •——•

Q ——•—

R •—•

S •••

T —

U ••—

V •••—

W •——

X —••—

Y —•——

Z ——••

 Share Morse code with up to four friends!
Use the Decoder Cards from the back of this book.

Decode this Coconut message:

•••/••••/•—/•—•/••/—•/——•

___ ___ ___ ___ ___ ___ ___

•——/••/—/••••

___ ___ ___ ___

•—

___

••—•/•—•/••/•/—•/—••

___ ___ ___ ___ ___ ___

—••/———/••—/—•••/•—••/•/•••

___ ___ ___ ___ ___ ___ ___

—•——/———/••—/•—•

___ ___ ___ ___

••—•/••—/—•

___ ___ ___

23

Cocoa Code

Here's another way to send your friend a mysterious message. Rub a sheet of paper with a white candle. Lay the paper wax-side down on a blank sheet of paper. Write on the back of the waxed sheet, pressing firmly. The message is now written on the "blank" paper. To see the message, have a friend sprinkle it with cocoa! (Do this somewhere that's easy to clean up, like the kitchen sink.)

Here are some fun messages to try
with the Cocoa Code:

Life is full of sweet
surprises.

A good friend is the
sweetest treat.

Switcheroo

Write the alphabet in lowercase letters. Starting any-where, write the alphabet below it in capital letters. We started under the lowercase "s." To use the code, find a letter on the top line but write the one on the bottom line.

a	b	c	d	e	f	g
I	J	K	L	M	N	O

h	i	j	k	l	m	n
P	Q	R	S	T	U	V

o	p	q	r	s	t	u
W	X	Y	Z	A	B	C

v	w	x	y	z
D	E	F	G	H

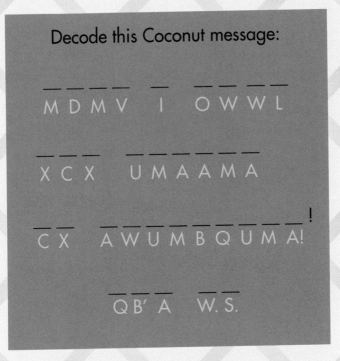

Decode this Coconut message:

_ _ _ _   _   _ _ _ _
M D M V   I   O W L

_ _ _   _ _ _ _ _ _
X C X   U M A A M A

_ _   _ _ _ _ _ _ _ _!
C X   A W U M B Q U M A!

_ _ _ _   _ _ _
Q B' A   W. S.

 Share this version of Switcheroo with up to four friends!
Use the Decoder Cards from the back of this book.

Tiny Type

This trick works well when you're sending a message that's so little, it can fit inside small places, like a fortune cookie, a tiny pocket, or the cap of a pen. All you have to do is write as small as you can!

Here's a tiny message for you:

It takes a big friend to forgive little problems.

The Secret Strips in the back of the Code Book are perfect for writing Tiny Type messages.

Fake Finales

A *finale* (fi-NAH-lay) is an ending or a big finish. For this quick code, you add a false letter to the end of each word.

Itz makesp theb wordsu looko funnya andi hardu top readl.

Decode this Coconut message:

Tod geth whata youv wantr, keepb diggingh.

Cracking the Codes!

Page 5: Start every day wagging your tail. **7:** Practicing with a friend makes anything more fun! **9:** A duck because it can quack the codes! **13:** A true friend sticks by your side. **15:** Friends are everywhere—you just have to look. **17:** Always lend a helping paw. **19:** Friendship makes life paws-itively great! **21:** Friends are golden. **23:** Sharing with a friend doubles your fun. **27:** Even a good pup messes up sometimes! **30:** To get what you want, keep digging. It's O.K.

Decoder Cards

Give a decoder card to a friend so that she can crack your coded messages. There are four copies of each of these cards, so you can share with several buddies! Carefully tear out each card.

Doodle Decoder

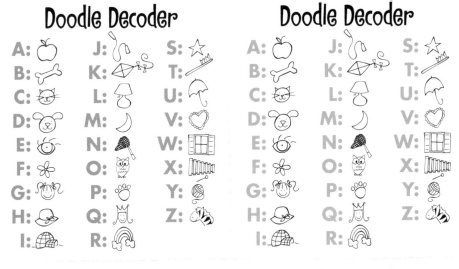

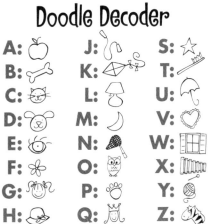

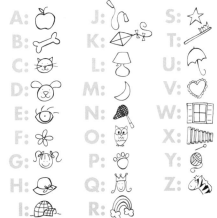

By the Numbers

A	B	C	D	E	F	G
20	21	22	23	24	25	26

H	I	J	K	L	M	N
1	2	3	4	5	6	7

O	P	Q	R	S	T	U
8	9	10	11	12	13	14

V	W	X	Y	Z
15	16	17	18	19

By the Numbers

A	B	C	D	E	F	G
20	21	22	23	24	25	26

H	I	J	K	L	M	N
1	2	3	4	5	6	7

O	P	Q	R	S	T	U
8	9	10	11	12	13	14

V	W	X	Y	Z
15	16	17	18	19

By the Numbers

A	B	C	D	E	F	G
20	21	22	23	24	25	26

H	I	J	K	L	M	N
1	2	3	4	5	6	7

O	P	Q	R	S	T	U
8	9	10	11	12	13	14

V	W	X	Y	Z
15	16	17	18	19

By the Numbers

A	B	C	D	E	F	G
20	21	22	23	24	25	26

H	I	J	K	L	M	N
1	2	3	4	5	6	7

O	P	Q	R	S	T	U
8	9	10	11	12	13	14

V	W	X	Y	Z
15	16	17	18	19

Puzzling Pattern

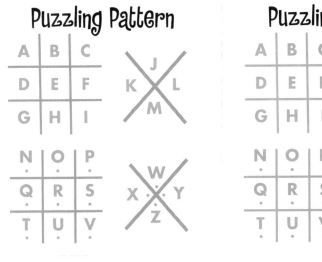

Puzzling Pattern

Puzzling Pattern

Puzzling Pattern

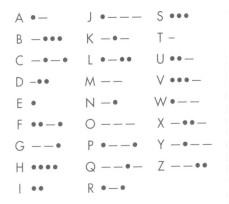

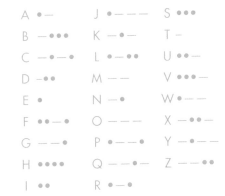
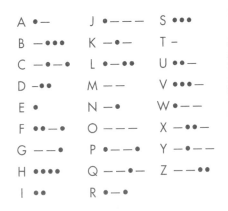

Coconut ™ Top-Secret Codes

Coconut ™ Top-Secret Codes

Coconut ™ Top-Secret Codes

Coconut ™ Top-Secret Codes

Coconut ™ Top-Secret Codes

Coconut ™ Top-Secret Codes

Coconut ™ Top-Secret Codes

Coconut ™ Top-Secret Codes

Coconut ™ Top-Secret Codes

Coconut ™ Top-Secret Codes

Coconut ™ Top-Secret Codes

Coconut ™ Top-Secret Codes

Coconut ™ Top-Secret Codes

Coconut ™ Top-Secret Codes

Coconut ™ Top-Secret Codes

Coconut ™ Top-Secret Codes

Coconut ™ Top-Secret Codes

Coconut ™ Top-Secret Codes

Coconut ™ Top-Secret Codes

Coconut ™ Top-Secret Codes

Switcheroo

a	b	c	d	e	f	g
I	J	K	L	M	N	O

h	i	j	k	l	m	n
P	Q	R	S	T	U	V

o	p	q	r	s	t	u
W	X	Y	Z	A	B	C

v	w	x	y	z
D	E	F	G	H

Switcheroo

a	b	c	d	e	f	g
I	J	K	L	M	N	O

h	i	j	k	l	m	n
P	Q	R	S	T	U	V

o	p	q	r	s	t	u
W	X	Y	Z	A	B	C

v	w	x	y	z
D	E	F	G	H

Switcheroo

a	b	c	d	e	f	g
I	J	K	L	M	N	O

h	i	j	k	l	m	n
P	Q	R	S	T	U	V

o	p	q	r	s	t	u
W	X	Y	Z	A	B	C

v	w	x	y	z
D	E	F	G	H

Switcheroo

a	b	c	d	e	f	g
I	J	K	L	M	N	O

h	i	j	k	l	m	n
P	Q	R	S	T	U	V

o	p	q	r	s	t	u
W	X	Y	Z	A	B	C

v	w	x	y	z
D	E	F	G	H

Coconut™

Top-Secret
Codes

Coconut™

Top-Secret
Codes

Coconut™

Top-Secret
Codes

Coconut™

Top-Secret
Codes

Write a tiny message on a **Secret Strip!**
Carefully tear out along each strip.

Here are some other Coconut books you might like:

❑ I read it.

❑ I read it.

❑ I read it.

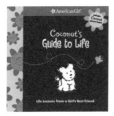

❑ I read it.

❑ I read it.

❑ I read it.

Send us a message in code—
but don't forget to tell us which code you're using!

Write to:

Top-Secret Codes Editor
American Girl
P.O. Box 620998
8400 Fairway Place
Middleton, WI 53562